I SPY ANIMALS!

I SPY with my little eye, something beginning with...

C is for
CRAB!

I SPY with my little eye, something beginning with...

K is for KANGAROO!

I SPY with my little eye, something beginning with...

 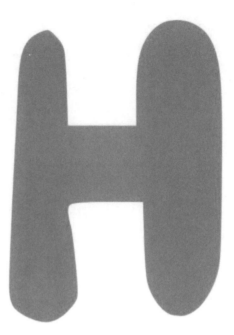

is for

HIPPO!

I SPY with my little eye, something beginning with...

P

is for

PEACOCK!

I SPY with my little eye, something beginning with...

I SPY with my little eye, something beginning with...

D is for **DUCK!**

I SPY with my little eye, something beginning with...

is for

OCTOPUS!

I SPY with my little eye, something beginning with...

A
is for
ANT!

I SPY with my little eye, something beginning with...

G is for GIRAFFE!

I SPY with my little eye, something beginning with...

E is for
ELEPHANT!

I SPY with my little eye, something beginning with...

Z
is for
ZEBRA!

I SPY with my little eye, something beginning with...

R is for RABBIT!

I SPY with my little eye, something beginning with...

is for

SHEEP!

I SPY with my little eye, something beginning with...

J is for JELLYFISH!

I SPY with my little eye, something beginning with...

B
is for
BUTTERFLY!

I SPY with my little eye, something beginning with...

M is for
MONKEY!

I SPY with my little eye, something beginning with...

T is for TIGER!

I SPY with my little eye, something beginning with...

is for

FROG!

I SPY BOOKS
for preschoolers

Find us on Amazon!

Discover all of the titles available in the series;
including these below...

I SPY IN THE COUNTRYSIDE!

I SPY IN THE CITY!

I SPY AT THE SEASIDE!

I SPY CHARACTERS & TOYS!

I SPY EVERYTHING!

I SPY FROM A-Z!

You'll also love;

I SPY – Color the A-Z!

Featuring puzzles for each letter of the alphabet, this book is also a coloring book!

© 2018 Webber Books

Images and vectors by;

freepix, alekksall, art.shcherbyna, agnessz_arts, anggar3ind, Alliesinteractive, Anindyanfitri, Ajipebriana, Alliesinteractive, Balasoui, Bakar015, Bimbimkha, brgfx, cornecoba, creativepack, creativetoons, ddraw, dooder, drawnhy97, elsystudio, Emily_b, flaticon, freshgraphix, frimufilms, Garrykillian, gordoba, graphicrepublic, graphicmama, iconicbestiary, ibrandify, Jannoon028, johndory, Kamimiart, kat_branch, kbibibi, Kjpargeter, Kraphix, layerace, lesyaskripak, lexamer, lyolya_profitrolya, Macrovector, Makyzz, milano83, Miguel_ruiz, nenilkime, natalka_dmitrova, natkacheva, omegapics, Pickapic, rawpixel, Rayzong, renata.s, rezzaalam, rocketpixel, RosaPuchalt, Rwdd_studios, sketchepedia, stephanie2212, SilviaNatalia, Terdpongvector, titusurya, vectorpocket, Vectortwins, Vector4free, vectorportal, vectorpouch, vecteezy, VVstudio, Visnezh, zirconicusso

Made in the USA
Monee, IL
30 March 2020